SHORT · SCENIC · WALKS
TEESDALE & WEARDALE

PAUL HANNON

HILLSIDE PUBLICATIONS
2 New School Lane, Cullingworth, Bradford BD13 5DA

First Published 2021   © Paul Hannon 2021

ISBN 978 1 907626 35 7

While the author has walked and researched all these routes for the purposes of this guide, no responsibility can be accepted for any unforeseen circumstances encountered whilst following them

Sketch maps based on OS 1947 1-inch maps

Cover illustrations: Barnard Castle; Low Force
Back cover: Bollihope; Page 1: High Force
(Paul Hannon/Yorkshire Photo Library)

Printed in China on behalf of Latitude Press

HILLSIDE GUIDES... cover much of Northern England

- 50 Yorkshire Walks For All
- Journey of the Wharfe (photobook)

Short Scenic Walks
- Teesdale & Weardale
- Ribble Valley & Bowland
- Wharfedale & Ilkley
- Three Peaks & Malham
- North York Moors
- Harrogate & Nidderdale
- Wensleydale & Swaledale
- Ambleside & South Lakeland
- Arnside & Lunesdale
- Aire Valley
- Haworth
- Hebden Bridge
- Around Pendle

Walking in Yorkshire
- North York Moors South & West
- Nidderdale & Ripon
- Wharfedale & Malham
- Aire Valley & Bronte Country
- Yorkshire Wolds
- South Yorkshire
- Three Peaks & Howgill Fells
- North York Moors North & East
- Wensleydale & Swaledale
- Harrogate & Ilkley
- Howardian Hills & Vale of York
- Calderdale & South Pennines
- West Yorkshire Countryside

Lancashire/Cumbria/North Pennines
- Pendle & the Ribble
- Eden Valley

Visit us at www.hillsidepublications.co.uk

CONTENTS

Harwood Beck
Ireshopeburn chapel

Introduction..........................4

1 Egglestone Abbey........... 6
2 Flatts Wood................... 8
3 Around Cotherstone......10
4 Currack Rigg.................12
5 Baldersdale...................14
6 Goldsborough...............16
7 Hury Reservoir..............18
8 Fairy Cupboards...........20
9 Egglesburn...................22
10 Tees at Middleton........ 24
11 Kirkcarrion...................26
12 Hudes Hope.................28
13 Around Newbiggin.......30
14 Low Force.................... 32
15 Holwick Scars...............34
16 High Force...................36
17 Langdon Beck...............38
18 Cauldron Snout.............40
19 Wearhead.....................42
20 Ireshopeburn.................44
21 Middlehope Burn..........46
22 Rookhope Arch.............48
23 Boltslaw Incline............50
24 Rookhope Burn.............52
25 Stanhope Burn..............54
26 Bollihope Landscapes...56
27 Tunstall Reservoir..........58
28 Wear at Wolsingham.....60
29 Hamsterley Forest......... 62
30 Grassholme Reservoir....64

INTRODUCTION

The North Pennines Area of Outstanding Natural Beauty boasts Teesdale as is its best-known valley, supported by neighbouring Weardale. The rivers Tees and Wear run similar courses between high moorland skylines, and each has many deep-cut side valleys and a string of interesting villages. A riverbank stroll quickly reveals the beauty of the Tees, though the only places that see visitors in any numbers are High and Low Forces. Weardale remains relatively unknown, yet its unassuming charms also include some splendid riverbank walking. Teesdale's major side valleys flow in from the west, the rivers Lune and Balder creating the local lakeland, with five large reservoirs adding their own attraction to the area.

Only when one ventures onto the open moors, or into the almost hidden side valleys, does one discover the ravages of lead mining. During the 18th and 19th centuries these quiet scenes echoed to the sound of industry, though evocative ruins, spoil heaps, scars and shafts are all that survive. Finest visible remains are at the Killhope museum at the head of Weardale, but many sites are passed on these walks. Literary connections link both Charles Dickens and Sir Walter Scott with Teesdale, while the artist Turner also turned his attention to the local scenery.

The majority of walks are on rights of way or established access areas and paths: a handful which cross Open Access land are noted as such. Most days of the year you can freely walk here, but dogs are banned from grouse moors other than on rights of way. These areas can occasionally be closed, most likely from the grouse-shooting season's August start, though weekends should largely be unaffected: details from Natural England and information centres. Whilst the route description should be sufficient to guide you around, a map is recommended for greater information and interest: Ordnance Survey Explorer maps OL31, OL19 & 307 cover the walks.

- North Pennines AONB Partnership, Weardale Business Centre, 1 Martin Street, Stanhope DL13 2UY (01388-528801)
- 3 Horsemarket **Barnard Castle** DL12 8LY (03000-262626)
- Visitor Information, 10 Market Place **Middleton-in-Teesdale** DL12 0QG (01833-641001)
- Visitor Centre **Bowlees** DL12 0XE (03000-262626)
- Durham Dales Centre **Stanhope** DL13 2FJ (03000-262626)

TEESDALE & WEARDALE
30 Short Scenic Walks

Romaldkirk

1 EGGLESTONE ABBEY

3¾ miles from Barnard Castle

A simple stroll close by the River Tees to a monastic gem

Start *Buttermarket (NZ 050163; DL12 8NQ), car parks*
Map *OS Explorer OL31, North Pennines - Teesdale & Weardale*

For a note on Barnard Castle see page 8. From the Buttermarket descend the main road (The Bank), passing Blagraves, oldest house in town. When it swings right, continue straight down Thorngate, where some fine old houses lead to the now residential Thorngate Mill. Alongside is Thorngate Bridge, a large footbridge on the River Tees. Across, go left with the river, a firm path passing houses and a weir into more open surrounds, soon arriving at a vast caravan site at River View Park (Lendings). On entering, advance very briefly towards a site road junction, and turn right steeply uphill. Swinging left at the top, it quickly rises out of the site. Part way up, a kissing-gate on the left sends a grassy path away across grassy pastures. Remain on this for some time above the site, then on above the wooded bank of the river to ultimately reach a stile in a hedge at the end onto Abbey Lane.

Go left to quickly reach Bow Bridge, a sidelined 17th century packhorse bridge on Thorsgill Beck. A few yards further a gate on the right sends a grassy path away beneath Egglestone Abbey. A short way on, a path doubles back left up the bank to a lone cottage, quickly revealing the abbey just ahead. With further dwellings at Abbey Farm to your right, the path crosses to the abbey car park. Egglestone Abbey is in the care of English Heritage, and occupies a lovely spot. It is normally open, free of charge, at all reasonable times. It was founded by Ralph de Malton for Premonstratensian canons ('White Canons') from Easby, near

Richmond in 1196, and though constantly in financial turmoil, it survived until the Dissolution in 1538.

Leave by the access road dropping back to the road, and advance a short way further to a junction at the splendid arch of Abbey Bridge (1773) spanning Abbey Gorge: here the river races through rock walls of a grey limestone, Teesdale Marble. Across, a stile on the left sends a path upstream through trees above the lively river. Quickly reaching a kissing-gate into grassy pasture, advance for a lengthy spell along the bank, a lovely stroll with limestone scars over to the right. Later becoming confined, you emerge past sewage works into another pasture. At the end of this pass through a fence gap and resume in a last pasture to become enclosed at a bridle-gate to reach renovated Demesne Mill and cottages. Follow the access road out into an open public space to run on to Gray Lane to rejoin the junction at the foot of The Bank.

Either return up it, or preferable go across past the Blue Bell pub and along Bridgegate past an old milestone to County Bridge on the Tees beneath the castle. Don't cross the bridge but take a surfaced path on the right beneath the castle walls, at the end of which swing right up onto an open green by the castle entrance. Just along to the right is the town centre road bend where Galgate meets the Market Place.

Egglestone Abbey

2 FLATTS WOOD

4¼ miles from Barnard Castle

Largely woodland walking on good paths by the Tees

Start Buttermarket (NZ 050163; DL12 8NQ), car parks
Map OS Explorer OL31, North Pennines - Teesdale & Weardale

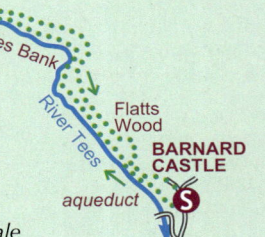

Barnard Castle - 'Barney' - is the hub of Teesdale, its bustling market place climbing to the broad sweep of Galgate and Bernard's Castle on its cliff-top perch above the river. Founded around 1100, it has faced siege in various centuries. The market cross, or Buttermarket, is the highly individual building in the lower market place. Built in 1747, it has served as court, jail and town hall. Opposite is St Mary's church, late 12th to early 14th century. Dickens stayed at the Kings Head in 1838 while researching for Nicholas Nickleby. Most visitors seek out the Bowes Museum on the edge of town: its remarkable facade fronts the late 19th century house of John Bowes, Earl of Strathmore.

From the Buttermarket head north on the broad Market Place to the junction with Galgate. Here go left past the Methodist church into a popular grassy sward by the castle. Remain on the main surfaced path slanting right down into trees, dropping to the Tees at a weir. Just upstream is a river footbridge, the Tees Aqueduct. Don't cross, but head upstream through Flatts Wood, bridging Percy Beck to enter a clearing. Your path will remain near the river now for a considerable time, with little description needed as the path ambles pleasurably along the richly wooded bank.

Initially a broad carriageway, the path later becomes more varied. When a right fork sends stone steps up towards an old viaduct, remain by the river with a glimpse of its forlorn abutment above. The Tees Viaduct was built in 1861 and demolished in

1972, its four tall piers conveying the line to Kirkby Stephen via Stainmore: across the other side, the Middleton branch departed. Your path undertakes several minor rises and falls, then a lower level stroll precedes a super section tight by the Tees beneath rocky scars, with golden cliffs on the very bank. Steps climb back out, and things open out for a sustained level sect on to finally reach a gate into a contrastingly open sheep pasture by the lush riverbank.

Forsaking the Tees, the onward route follows the wall briefly to a bridle-gate, then ascends steeply through trees, swinging right to one out of the wood. Take the path right to begin the return, initially by arable fields. A wall replaces the fence before reaching a gate into the trees, from where a super path runs inside the wood top. Lush sheep pastures replace crops to your left, and ultimately you arrive at the old railway: a kink deflects you right into the wood top at the site of the old viaduct. Of two paths heading left, take the upper one to resume as before, finally reaching a bend where the path slants right down through the trees. At a near immediate fork, keep left to slant down to meet a level path at the bottom in front of Percy Beck. Go briefly left to cross a footbridge on it, then a steep, initially stone-stepped path rises away to emerge onto the end of suburban Raby Avenue. Head away along this, kinking left at the end to go the short way further back to the town centre.

The Bowes Museum, Barnard Castle

3   AROUND COTHERSTONE

3½ miles from Cotherstone

Easy rambling around the charming environs of a lovely village

Start *Village centre (NZ 010198; DL12 9PF), The Hagg parking area down lane opposite Fox & Hounds*
Map *OS Explorer OL31, North Pennines - Teesdale & Weardale*

    Cotherstone is an attractive street village with a green at each end. St Cuthbert's church boasts a tall spire, while a Quaker meeting house dates from 1797. With your back to the Fox & Hounds, cross the main road and down an access road opposite. Quickly forking, go straight on past scattered houses, including one with a 1774 sundial. Ending on a knoll, to your left is the site of a castle dating from around 1200. Advance on, becoming a cart track dropping to end above a steep drop to the River Tees.

    Take the gate on the right by wooden sheds, past which is a bridle-gate on the left onto the wooded bank top. A super path runs on above a solitary grave and crosses the former Cotherstone Mill access road. Opening out a little further to join another access road, advance on this until it drops gently towards a house ahead. Here a part-flagged path slants left down an open bank to enter trees to reach a bridle-gate. With the river just below, the path advances on beneath quarried cliffs: when they end the path drops left near the river, briefly, to a kissing-gate into a flat pasture. A path runs to a footbridge on Lance Beck at the end, where you leave the Tees. The path slants up the bank to approach Cooper House, swinging right to a kissing-gate in a wall.

    Go left with the wall enclosing the grounds just as far as the access road, then follow it right across a field centre to a modern barn. From a stile in the wall that starts here, head away with a fence on your left to a stile at the end. Rising gently away, part way up take a stile in the adjacent fence, then rise slightly away from it to one in a fence ahead. Drop left the short way to a stony track as it bridges a streamlet, then advance on it across a field centre. At the end it swings right to cross the old ra lway, but strictly you rise the tiny way further to a gate accessing a bridge over the line. Immediately over, drop right to the other side of that gap. As the first section of the Railway Path is overgrown, pass through a gate just ahead and advance just a short way outside the line to reach a kissing-gate accessing it. At once a super path runs left, and this traces the dead-straight, richly foliaged line to ultimately drop onto the road on the village edge.

Go left a few yards to a stile opposite, before a bridge. A path crosses to a small gate in the hedge ahead, bears right with the fence, then left past the old station to a corner stile onto the line. Cross over to an enclosed path heading away to meet an access road, with playing fields on your right. Just two yards right resume on a grassy way to a wall-stile in front, on outside the church to emerge onto an access road. Advance the short way to the main road, and cross straight over to Hawcroft Lane heading away past houses. At the first chance an inviting green way runs left between gardens the short way out onto East Green, with its attractive Georgian houses. From its far corner advance along the main road past the Red Lion back to the start.

East Green, Cotherstone

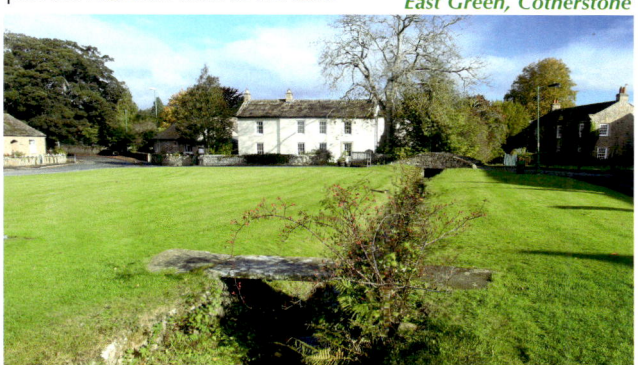

4   CURRACK RIGG

4¼ miles from Cotherstone

Grassy moorland, railway and fieldpaths

Start *Village centre (NZ 010198;*
DL12 9PF), The Hagg parking area
down lane opposite Fox & Hounds
Map *OS Explorer OL31,*
North Pennines - Teesdale & Weardale

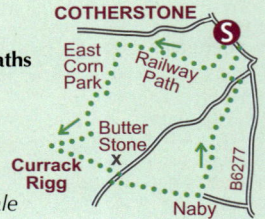

For a note on Cotherstone see page 10. With your back to the Fox & Hounds go right a few strides, and turn right on an access road. Quickly reaching a junction before a sharp bend left, take a back lane right along the rear of houses. At the pub car park a stile on the left sends a nice path up a long field centre to a stile onto the old Tees Valley Railway. Turn right on the Railway Path, a fine stride that passes beneath a substantial arched bridge before reaching a gate onto a rough access road. Go left, ascending to a cattle-grid then rising more steeply to approach East Corn Park.

As it swings right to the house, a grass track bears left to a gate above the grounds. Through it rise left with the fence, veering right to a gate in the wall ahead. Advance to a gentle brow just ahead, then drop to another wall-gate onto a corner of Currack Rigg's grassy moorland. Over a wooden bridge on Crook Beck bear left, down over a streamlet from where a trod slants briefly steeply left up to an outer wall corner. Just ten yards above, a thin but clear path is joined. Go right to commence an imperceptible rise across the moor with a reedy groove to your right. This runs a good course to level out alongside the streamlet, just past which you meet a grassy track fording the stream.

Don't cross but double back left up the track, easing out to run a super course along to a moorland road, with the Butter Stone down to your left just before it. This is a 17th century plague stone, where money for produce was disinfected by placing it in vinegar in hollows in the top. Turn briefly right up the road to a gentle brow, then go left on a grassy bridleway dropping slightly to a wall-gate off the moor into a field. Head away, picking up a farm track that runs to a gate at the end. It then runs enclosed the short way to the farm at Naby. Midway along the yard, go left between stone barns, passing modern barns to a gate, then down to two further gates. To your right is an extensive water treatment works.

The track drops down a field to end through another gate with a barn to the left. Your way is straight down the field with an old line of trees to your right, reaching a fence-stile on the right just short of the corner. Bear gently away down the next field, dropping through a line of trees to a small bridge. Across, advance the short way to a corner gate in front of houses, resuming with the wall outside the gardens. At the end pass through a broad hedge-gap and drop to cross to a stile onto the Railway Path. Cross to another into a small field, with the church spire ahead. Drop to a gate hiding a wall-stile between houses. A snicket runs to an access road, with a tiny green to your left. Go left a few yards on the road, then right along a short access road past a few houses. Through a gate/stile at the end, advance a short way further to a wall-stile on the right. A path crosses stone slabs on a streamlet and descends the fieldside to a gate/stile onto a drive. Go straight ahead down to the main road just below, and left past the Red Lion to finish.

The Butter Stone

5   BALDERSDALE

$4\frac{1}{4}$ miles from Balder Head

A circuit of Blackton Reservoir with much added interest

Start Balderhead Reservoir (NY 928187; DL12 9UX), car park at north end of dam
Map OS Explorer OL31, North Pennines - Teesdale & Weardale
Access Water company permissive paths

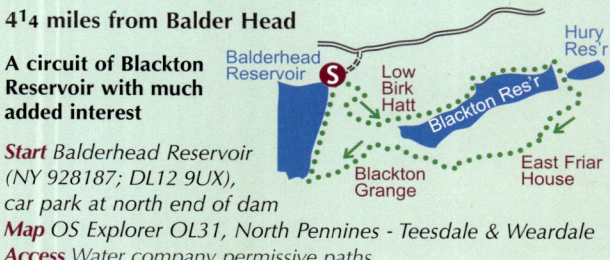

    Completed in 1965, Balderhead Reservoir sits 1082ft/330m up, highest of the trio of Baldersdale lakes. From the car park retrace steps a few yards and turn right down a stony access road. With Blackton Reservoir immediately below, this winds down the slope beneath the big grassy dam. Meeting the outflowing River Balder below, the track runs towards Blackton Bridge. Through the gate, don't cross the bridge but turn left on an inviting grassy way above the reedy reservoir head. It soon rises slightly to a large gate in front of Low Birk Hatt. This was home to Hannah Hauxwell, who became an unlikely celebrity after the 1972 documentary 'Too Long A Winter' captivated a Yorkshire Television audience with the enduring story of her arduous farming life.

    Don't pass through but take a gate on the right onto Blackton Reservoir's north shore path, with a bird hide to your right. A grassy path heads away beneath the farm for an excellent stroll above the shore. A couple of minor inlets are bridged and the path veers right at the end to a gate in front of the dam, completed in 1896. Follow the access road across it, looking down on Hury Reservoir with shapely Goldsborough ahead. At the end remain briefly on the stony road to bridge a sidestream with a waterfall upstream. Across, take a wall-stile on the right to rise briefly with a wall above the now tame stream. At a bend in the wall bear right to cross the stream to a wall-stile just before wall and stream meet.

Entering new tree plantings, rise slightly to a fence-stile just above, then rise left and cross to a gate right of a barn. Now bear left to a gate in a dip half way along the wall. As you rise towards East Friar House, bear right to a gate in the wall, and slant up to the top wall. Go right, and this remains your largely pathless course at or near the top of several fields via a string of stiles. The Balderhead dam becomes more prominent ahead, then Blackton Reservoir finally re-appears. Faced with a wood just ahead, bear sharply right to drop between woods to a farm bridge on a stream.

A brief green way rises up the other side, and from the fence corner a thin path bears left to a wall-stile opposite. Bear right down to a wall-stile half way along, then left to a guidepost by a descending track. Turn down it to a gate and bridge on Hunder Beck. Just a little further the track swings right back to Blackton Bridge, but instead take the inviting grassy track rising left to a gate, then equally nicely up to Blackton Grange (a hostel). Advance to its rough access road rising way, on through a wall-gate then more stonily up to a junction at a parking area at the south end of the Balderhead dam. Turn right to follow the road the length of the dam to finish, with both reservoirs down-dale also in view.

Low Birk Hatt, Blackton Reservoir

6 GOLDSBOROUGH

4¼ miles from Hury

Excellent grassy moorland paths to a Teesdale landmark

Start *Hury Reservoir (NY 966192; DL12 9UP), water company car park at south end of dam*
Map *OS Explorer OL31, North Pennines - Teesdale & Weardale*
Access *Open Access, see page 4*

Completed in 1894 by Tees Valley Water Board, Hury is the oldest of Teesdale's five reservoirs, and is a popular trout fishery: the hamlet of Hury stands above the north bank. Rejoin the road alongside the old keeper's house, and go left just as far as a bend. Here take the farm drive on the right, but leave at once by a gate on the left. Cross to the right-hand of two gates opposite, then on to a corner wall-stile. Just beyond is a stile into Keepers Cottage. Turn right up the drive to a wall-stile onto a road, then right to its early demise at Fiddler House. A fence-gate to its right puts you onto a corner of Goldsborough Rigg, with Goldsborough ahead.

Of two grassy ways rising away, take the right one and remain on it for a superb, gentle ascent across the moor. Within minutes keep right when a left branch makes for the deep confines of How Beck, while a little further you cross a wooden bridge on a streamlet. Eventually, on reaching zones of bracken, the way levels out and shortly forks. Take the left branch, an initially level, grassy track entering bracken and winding down past a circular sheepfold to ford the little stream. The grassy way steeply ascends the opposite bank between bracken, quickly easing and running gently up to a gate at a wall corner outside MOD property.

Small trods go right from both the gate and the wall corner: yours is that heading south-west from the gate, declining slightly then soon rising slightly to a waymarked T-junction. Joining the

Pennine Way's seldom trodden Bowes Loop, go right to quickly reach an odd metal footbridge at How Beck Head. Across, it rises slightly on a bee-line for Goldsborough. The path swings left round the base of the crags, though many will be tempted to inspect them more closely. Goldsborough's gritstone rocks offer sweeping views, with the massif of Mickle Fell prominent across Baldersdale. The path quickly reaches a brow with all three Baldersdale reservoirs in view. As it starts to descend it quickly forks: take the broader right branch directly down the moor to join an unfenced road.

Go right, gently downhill to swing left at a cattle-grid off the moor. A little lower, take an invisible path signed right, crossing to a corner wall-stile. Head away across a larger pasture, merging with the wall below to reach a corner stile/gate. Advance on the field bottom past a house at Scoon Bank (gate/stile) and on to a couple of barns. At the second take a gate to resume on the other side, and head away on a direct march through a string of fields (with gates and sometimes stiles too), with the boundary on your right and the reservoir below across the minor road. After a slender field crossing, head past a large barn and field centre, with West Briscoe farm below. A wall returns to lead on to a corner stile over a plank bridge. Cross one final paddock to a gate at another West Briscoe: go left the short way down the drive to rejoin your outward route at the road, with the finish two minutes to the left.

Goldsborough

7   HURY RESERVOIR

4 miles from Hury

A simple reservoir circuit on cushioned grassy paths

Start *Hury (NY 965197; DL12 9UR), water company car park at north end of dam*
Map *OS Explorer OL31, North Pennines - Teesdale & Weardale*
Access *Water company permissive paths*

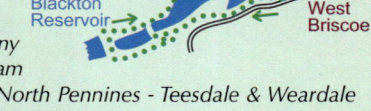

Completed in 1894 by the Tees Valley Water Board, Hury is the oldest of the five reservoirs in Teesdale's lakeland. It covers 125 acres, with a maximum depth of 90ft, and also operates as a popular trout fishery. The farm across the road, once an inn, is still marked on maps as Strathmore Arms. The hamlet of Hury stands high above the north bank, and a century ago included the Hare & Hounds Inn and a Wesleyan Chapel.

Return to a gate at the grassy dam and cross to the far side, enjoying big views across to Goldsborough and the more distant Shacklesborough. Alongside the former reservoir keeper's house, don't join the road but turn right through a small car park. Just beyond it a metal footbridge takes you over the massive concrete by-wash channel carrying surplus water from the reservoirs up-dale. At once a grassy path heads off westwards along the bank, running a splendid, uncomplicated course along the full length of the southern shore. Part way on, a promontory is ignored as the path remains with the adjacent fence and by-wash, the shore returning at a gate at a small inlet. The grassy dam of Blackton Reservoir is revealed ahead as you run to a gate onto a bridleway alongside a metal by-wash bridge on your left and embankment on your right. In front is a subsidiary dam. Note that simply crossing the embankment here would reduce the distance to three miles.

Preferably, cross the bridge on your left and take the grassy track slanting left the short way up to a gate onto an access road. Turn right on this for a level stroll above a wooded bank: quickly bridging a sidestream, note the waterfall n its ravine on your left. The track swings right to reach the dam of Blackton Reservoir, completed in 1896. Cross it, noting yet another grassy dam, that of Balderhead Reservoir further up-dale. At the far side, drop right to a bridle-gate in a fence where it meets the sturdy reservoir wall. A grassy path runs along beneath the wall to reach the north end of the subsidiary embankment.

Here commence your return along the north shore, with the wall as constant company. From a gate in front the first stage rises above a wooded bank, then on the shore to swing in to a substantial side arm. Here you cross a footbridge on the inflow, and slant right up the low bank behind to resume to the right, back out to the main body of the reservoir. Further on, a smaller inlet is crossed by a wide wooden bridge, doubling back to a fence-gate at the outer wall corner. The final stage runs through waterside rushes and often among throngs of anglers to a gate back into the car park.

Hury Reservoir

8 FAIRY CUPBOARDS

4½ miles from Romaldkirk

A charming village is gateway to paths by a lovely wooded riverbank and a wildflower-rich old railway

Start Village centre (NY 995220; DL12 9ED), roadside parking
Map OS Explorer OL31, North Pennines - Teesdale & Weardale

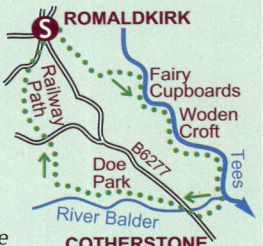

Romaldkirk is a tranquil place with a remarkable array of spacious greens. Focal point is St Romald's church: dating from the 12th century, inside is a 1304 effigy of Sir Hugh Fitzhenry. The imposing Rose & Crown also overlooks the greens across from the homely Kirk Inn. From the bend outside the church take a short access road between greens left of the Kirk Inn. Quickly reaching a junction go straight across between cottages, a short access track sending the enclosed path of Sennings Lane continuing on. This runs a lengthy, leafy course to ultimately end at a pair of gates. From the left one a path bears away across a field, crossing to a small gate, then more faintly at the same angle to a stile in a hedge. Drop onto a grassy way down to the derelict farm of Low Garth.

From a stile/gate to its right, a thin path bears left down the fieldside, swinging right to run above a wood to a gate/stile into trees. A path heads away above the Tees, dropping to a lively reach at Fairy Cupboards - small caves in riverbank ledges occupying a wonderful setting. The path later slants up to a stile/gate out of the wood, then left to another stile/gate. Continue to the buildings at Woden Croft, one of the infamous 'Yorkshire Schools' researched by Dickens for Nicholas Nickleby. In the yard go straight on past two houses on your left, and from a gate at the end turn down the field to a gate. A short enclosed section leads out into a field. A path forms as you bear gently right, down past a tree-lined stream to swing right to a kissing-gate in the corner, back with the river.

Over a footbridge on Wilden Beck, a briefly enclosed path leads to a kissing-gate out into a large, rolling pasture. A nice path crosses to another such gate back into trees at the far end, and a firm path runs on with the river. Passing an iron footbridge on the Tees you quickly reach a confluence with the River Balder. Here the path swings in to a footbridge on the latter, and with the steep knoll of Cotherstone Castle in front, the surfaced path runs right to a parking area at The Hagg on the edge of Cotherstone. Briefly follow the access road rising away, but leave at a gate on the right after a private drive. A muddy path runs towards the house, then improves to swing left parallel with the Balder. Scaling wooden steps at a pipeline, advance the short way further to a stile onto the B6277.

Go right over Balder Bridge to a stile on the left, and a nice path heads away, slanting up to a wooded bank. Through a gate it levels out with the 300-year old house of Doe Park to your right. Go left through a bridle-gate and on to a gate with a caravan site on your right. An enclosed section leads to a gate out of the site, then forge on outside the steep Balder Bank Woods on your left. Through several pastures Balder Viaduct appears to the left, and with the wood ended the last field is crossed to a kissing-gate onto a cutting of the old Tees Valley railway. Turn right for a super stroll on the Railway Path, crossing a country lane and delightfully on to ultimately rise to end at a road. Turn right to rejoin the B6277, crossing to the footway for a brief stroll back into the village.

The Tees at Fairy Cupboards

21

9 EGGLESBURN

4 miles from Eggleston

A wealth of interest, with a cameo visit to the Tees

Start Village centre (NY 999238; DL12 0AH), roadside parking
Map OS Explorer OL31, North Pennines - Teesdale & Weardale

Eggleston is a hillside village with 18th century Eggleston Hall Gardens open to the public, with café/shop. Holy Trinity church dates from 1869, while a Wesleyan chapel of 1828 has a Sunday school of 1881 attached. A Reading Room of 1887 is now the village hall with a modern war memorial, and across a neat green are the Three Tuns Inn and WC. Eggleston Show in September is the valley's major agricultural event. From the pub descend the street to a short access road on the right before the church, and part way on take a small gate on the left. A briefly enclosed path emerges onto a lawn and crosses to a footbridge in trees.

From a small gate behind, it runs briefly enclosed: keep on to emerge into a paddock ahead. Cross to a stile/gate in a wall to commence a level stroll beneath a fine series of lynchets, ancient cultivation terraces. Through a stile/gate at the end above a house, resume on its drive beneath further lynchets. Dropping to a cattle-grid and a drive junction, go left to another grid. A little further, leave the enclosed road at a gate on the right, crossing the field to a bridle-gate on the left just short of the end. Head away with Eggleston Burn to your right, and through a hedge-gap resume to drop to a corner stile onto the B6282 at Egglesburn Wood.

Go right over Egglesburn Bridge, then left on a cart track by a driveway. At once becoming a walled footway, its considerable course improves in quality to ultimately emerge at a bridle-gate into a field. Bear right to the nearest gate in the fence ahead, and follow a fence away to a corner gate. The other side of the hedge leads along to a big footbridge on the River Tees at Beckstones Wath. Don't cross but turn upstream to a bridle-gate into open pasture: a thin path resumes, rising slightly at the end to a gate. Here you leave the river for an old grassy way just ahead, doubling back up it to a gate. A largely level stroll then curves gently up and around to join an access road from Ornella barns. Go left up to a gate onto a drive at Toby Hill, and on a little further to emerge back onto the B6282 at a crossroads with a splendid seat at Egglesburn.

Cross and head up the road opposite, passing a Baptist Chapel of 1872, and on a few minutes further to a junction at a stone hut. This is the Saddle House, where spare saddles were kept for packhorses carrying lead ore to Blackton Smelt Mill. Turn right down a rough lane into trees to an idyllic scene at a footbridge and ford on Eggleston Burn. Beyond it you shortly cross a sidestream and rise to a junction outside Bendholm caravan park. Cross to a driveway ending at a cluster of houses at New Town. From a gate ahead, a splendid grassy path rises gently with a fence, with super views over the dale from above a bracken bank. Levelling out it runs to a gate at the end, though strictly the path uses a wall-stile just above. The other side leads to a garden wall corner and on with it to a stile/gate onto Balmer Lane at South Terrace. Go right to a junction with the B6278, and right again back into the centre.

Cottage garden at Eggleston

10   TEES AT MIDDLETON

3½ miles from Middleton-in-Teesdale

A lengthy riverside amid much interest on Middleton's fringe

Start Village centre (NY 947254; DL12 0SH), car parks
Map OS Explorer OL31, North Pennines - Teesdale & Weardale

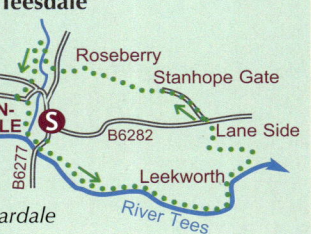

For a note on Middleton, see page 26. From the ornate iron fountain of 1877 – a legacy of lead mining days - turn down Bridge Street to the River Tees. Just before the bridge take an enclosed path left to commence a lengthy riverbank ramble. The way remains enclosed for a considerable time, with the Tees often obscured by a belt of attendant trees. Early features of interest include a setted section and a row of cottages with an intriguing shared garden. Beyond the outskirts you have sheep pastures alongside, and you encounter a dark, ravine-like section. Just beyond an extensive caravan site at Leekworth, a tapering enclosure leads to a kissing-gate into a field, and you finally leave the river.

Just a little further with a tree-lined streamlet in front, the path forks: bear left to a wall-stile just above, and briefly rise with the trees to your right. The path quickly bears left to run a straight, marginally rising course along a distinct little embankment. Passing through a tree-lined streamlet, turn sharp right up to a gate in the wall above, then slant left up to a corner stile/gate. The path rises by a garden edge onto the B6282 at Lane Side. Just a few yards left head up a narrow lane that eases out to terminate at Stanhope Gate. Pass through the farmyard, left of all the buildings to a grassy patch: drop left to a bridle-gate into the field ahead, ignoring an enclosed path to its left. Head away across the field to a gate, and on to a stile/gate ahead. Cross the next field to a stile/gate, and a wall leads along to Roseberry Cottage. Pass through the stile/gate into the yard and left along the enclosed driveway, which runs out to emerge at Town Head on the edge of the village. For a quick finish simply turn down here.

Ideally, cross to a cul-de-sac road (King's Walk) into trees opposite. Within a minute take a broad path slanting left down to a footbridge on Hudeshope Beck at a lovely waterfall. Across, rise to a broad track just ahead, and follow it left as it rises slightly to the wood top and on to a house. To its left a path runs out onto a road. Go right a few strides to the end of the buildings opposite, and an enclosed path heads away. First though, look back to see the Clock Tower by Middleton House, where the London Lead Company had their 19th century headquarters. The path drops down a fieldside to the bottom corner, then runs right to emerge onto the B6277: look back up the field for a good prospect of Middleton House.

Cross to the footway outside an old school opposite, and go briefly left to a bend. Here turn right on a short driveway, and when it swings right continue down a walled path dropping all the way to a path junction alongside Hudeshope Beck. Go left over the footbridge just yards from its confluence with the Tees, and the enclosed path runs the short way to emerge back at the bridge. Turn back up left to finish.

The fountain, Middleton

11 KIRKCARRION

3¼ miles from Middleton-in-Teesdale

Awesome green ways offer easy walking to and from a local landmark: massive views

Start Village centre (NY 947254; DL12 0SH), car parks
Map OS Explorer OL31, North Pennines - Teesdale & Weardale
Access Open Access (short section)

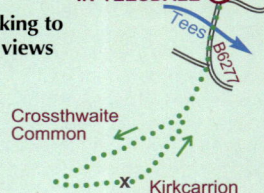

Middleton-in-Teesdale, capital of the upper dale, owes much to 19th century lead mining days, having been the headquarters of the London Lead Company. This Quaker-owned enterprise provided social and cultural facilities for their employees, and is credited as starting the country's first Co-operative movement here: families were provided for with education and healthcare. St Mary's church is resting place of Richard Watson the Teesdale Poet, and has a detached belfry of 1557. There are two pubs, shops, cafes and an information centre.

From the ornate iron fountain of 1877 - itself a legacy of lead mining days - turn down Bridge Street and cross Tees Bridge: the prominent wooded clump of Kirkcarrion hovers high ahead. Advance aon the footway past the auction mart up to a bend, where stood Middleton-in-Teesdale station, terminus of the Tees Valley railway. Go a few yards right along the Holwick lane and take a gate on the left (Pennine Way), from where a steep access track climbs away. Crossing the course of a mineral line that served a quarry up-dale, it transforms into a delectable grass track ascending the pasture towards Kirkcarrion. Rising to a gate in a wall to which you will return, big views look back over Middleton to the moors beyond Hudes Hope, also up-dale to Holwick Scars.

Through the gate the track swings right: immediately forking, keep to the right branch slanting up to a gate/stile in a fence. Through this, ignore a path straight ahead in favour of a broad, grassy way slanting right above a reedy groove. A gentle brow at the top proves to be a neat little 'ridge': dropping a few feet to a modest nick, it rises again across Crossthwaite Common. A briefly steeper rise through bracken leads to a momentary level point, where bear right on a thinner continuation path. It quickly rises more clearly to a cairn to ascend by a large rash of stones. From a cairn at the top, the final section rises to a gate in a wall above.

This is the walk's high point at some 1378ft/420m. Don't pass through, but leave the Pennine Way by going left with the wall, bound for Kirkcarrion. A good little trod traces the wall all the way, with several little dips to arrive at the circular wall enclosing the iconic pine plantation. Shown on old maps as Kirk Arran, the knoll contained a Bronze Age burial cairn, possibly of a local chieftain. From the wall corner around its left side, a grassy path descends through bracken near the wall. The path continues down the grassy common, broadening into an embanked way on the course of a 1½ miles-long tramway that served Greengates Quarry on the far side of Kirkcarrion. This ends abruptly at the wall lower down, but 50 yards before this point take a thin trod dropping left to join a broader path just short of a gate/stile in the fence from earlier. A green way continues down to merge with the outward route just above the wall-gate. Pass through to retrace steps back.

Kirkcarrion from above Middleton

12 HUDES HOPE

3½ miles from Coldberry

Exploring a colourful side valley with lead mining remains amid much else of interest

Start Hudes Hope (NY 944292; DL12 0QY), large beckside parking area 3 miles north of Middleton at northernmost point of Hudes Hope loop road
Map OS Explorer OL31, North Pennines - Teesdale & Weardale

● *roads to/from Middleton*

At the outset you are overlooked by the Coldberry Lead Mine, through which the walk will finish. For now cross the bridge on Hudeshope Beck, rising over a cattle-grid. Just past a drive on your left, bear off right at a footpath sign opposite a clump of scrub. An initially vague path drops a few feet then heads away, becoming clearer in rushes and bracken. Approaching a streamlet take the right fork, fading before reaching a kissing-gate in the wall ahead. A streamlet in a slim enclosure is crossed to a gate, with another gate ahead. A grassy continuation runs through bracken to pass left of a stone hut alongside a stone-arched level at Marlbeck Mine. The super grassy way runs on above the stream to a fence-gate, entering a larger site at the assorted ruins of High Skears Mine.

A broader green way continues, rising slightly to leave the site at a gate. It swings left and fades, but your way is straight on with the wall. This drops away, but your little path goes on above the wall to a stile ahead. With the plantation coming in below, a wall leads to a further stile, then the path drops slightly to run above the plantation wall to a stile into it just short of the end. A path along the wood top quickly descends steps to resume with a trench, passing Skears Quarry before dropping to the top of Parker's Kilns. Just beyond, branch right to inspect these three hugely impressive sets of twin kilns dating from 1840. Resume by dropping to the end of a surfaced road from Middleton just below.

Turn right on the continuing track across Miners Bridge, and a grassy path runs into Skears Plantation. A nice stroll upstream leads to a plank bridge on a sidestream by a mine level. Your onward route is up to the left, but first cautiously advance a short way on the forward path for a closer look at the splendid Skears Scars (or Jack Scar Gorge), where sheer limestone walls flank a rocky stream bed. The onward route climbs wooden steps and on to a stile out of the trees. A thin but clear path ascends the little bank, revealing open views of the upper reaches of your side valley. The thin path heads across pastures linked by wall-stiles. Part way along a larger one, the little path becomes briefly faint before crossing the grassy ravine of Clubgill Sike. From there a gentle slant leads up to a ladder-stile beneath the farm at Club Gill, with a final slant to a wall-stile onto a road.

Go briefly right over a cattle-grid, then bear left on an old mine road into the Coldberry Mine site to a sturdy building, Coldberry Shop. Dating from the 1820s, miners lodged here during their working week. This was a prolific lead mining area between the 18th and 19th centuries: on your left is the entrance to stone-arched Hunt's Level. Advance further on a grassy continuation past a crumbling barn to the start of a grassy embankment. Drop down its near side and gently descend open ground on the near side of a streamlet to join a track dropping back to the start.

Parker's Kilns

13   AROUND NEWBIGGIN

4¼ miles from Bowlees

Riverbank and pastures around a quaint old hamlet

Start *Visitor centre (NY 906281; DL12 0XF), car park off B6277*
Map *OS Explorer OL31, North Pennines - Teesdale & Weardale*

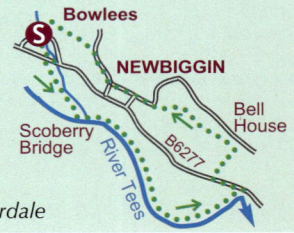

Based in an old Methodist chapel, Bowlees visitor centre has refreshments, a small shop and WC. It is linked to the car park by a footbridge on Bow Lee Beck. With your back to the centre, turn left along the old road the short way to the start of a wood on the right. Over a wall-gap a path runs downstream above Bow Lee Beck to a bridle-gate onto the B6277. A few yards to the right head down Banks access road opposite. Pass through the yard to a gate ahead, and a path runs on outside a plantation. Tapering to a gate at the end, the path curves right to a gate, and on to reach the River Tees at the footbridge of Scoberry Bridge, a lovely spot.

Don't cross but turn downstream to stiles either side of a footbridge on Bow Lee Beck, then resume with the Tees. This remains your course for some time through several stiles, the faint path improving as it enters more open terrain. Stiles and gates precede a section slightly away from the river to a gate at the end, then bearing right with an old wall to regain the river at a stile. A wall keeps the path confined to the bank, broadening out to take a kissing-gate at the end. Continuing grandly on above the little bank, a kissing-gate at the end puts you into a scrubby enclosure by the river. Soon entering trees, it runs on to shortly forsake the Tees, doubling back up a little bank to a stile back onto the B6277.

Turn left for a couple of minutes as far as a lone house, and take a drive rising right. When it swings left up towards Woodside Farm, continue up the side of a streamlet to a corner wall-stile. Resume up to another and then a third one: here the wall ends and you make a final ascent up a steep, scrubby pasture. At the top, locate a wall-stile behind scrub to emerge onto a level shelf. With Bell House just above, turn left with the wall, on through a gate to a stile on the left just before the corner. Its high-quality descent side is a place to sit and savour massive views. Slant away right down the pasture to a gate/stile, and advance on with a wall to a gate/stile into the wooded environs of Brockersgill Sike.

Advance briefly over the embankment, but as the main path slants further up, take a less obvious yet clear path dropping slightly on your left. This traverses a steep bank and on the short way to a stile out into a field. Bear left down to a stile opposite, then on to one in the wall below. Now drop right to a stile above a gate onto a narrow road on the edge of Newbiggin. Go left on this pleasant lane the length of this scattered hamlet. Part way on you pass a Methodist chapel of 1759, the oldest surviving in use in the country until closure in 2017. Keep on to a junction where a road drops left, and your onward one forks at open greens.

Take the Westgate road climbing left, soon leaving at a gate/stile set back on the left. A faint grass track crosses a sloping pasture to a gate/stile ahead, then on and down to a gate/stile at the rear of houses at Hood Gill. Head away in similar style with the wall on your left, and over a stile/gate a thin path crosses a broadening field centre to join a winding access track. Drop left down this the short way to a gate back into the car park.

Teesdale at Woodside Farm

14   LOW FORCE

4 miles from Bowlees

Easy walking dominated by a classic stroll by the lively River Tees

Start *Visitor centre (NY 906281; DL12 OXF), car park off B6277*
Map *OS OL31, North Pennines - Teesdale & Weardale*

    Based in an old Methodist chapel, Bowlees visitor centre is run by the North Pennines AONB, with refreshments, a small shop and WC. It is linked to the car park by a footbridge on Bow Lee Beck. With your back to the centre, turn left along the old road past cottages the short way to the start of a wood on the right. Over a wall-gap a path runs downstream above Bow Lee Beck to a bridle-gate onto the B6277. A few yards to the right head down Banks access road opposite. Pass through the yard to a gate ahead, and a grassy path runs on outside a plantation. Tapering to a gate at the end, the path curves right to a wall-gate, and on to reach the River Tees at the footbridge of Scoberry Bridge, a lovely spot.

    Cross and turn upstream on the Pennine Way, a very straightforward, lengthy riverbank stroll on a path that remains firm throughout. The Tees is regularly lively, with enchanting waterplay as you enter Upper Teesdale National Nature Reserve to suddenly arrive at Wynch Bridge. This famous suspension bridge dates from 1830, its 18th century predecessor being built to serve lead miners. Don't cross, but resume upstream to immediately survey the lovely setting of Low Force. This is a hugely popular spot with trippers, helped by its proximity to the road and a direct path from Bowlees. This busiest stage is quickly left behind as you pass through a bridle-gate and the path continues grandly on, with little changing as this high-quality riverbank ramble eventually brings you to the next footbridge, Holwick Head Bridge.

Cross and double back right on an enclosed track quickly rising to a gate back onto the B6277. From a stile opposite, slant right up the field to a brow and advance to an outer wall corner. Drop right of it to a gate onto a back road alongside white-walled Bridge House. Just a few yards right, a s im path drops the few yards through scrub to cross tiny Smithy Sike. From a stile behind, join a track rising from the farm at West Fr ar House on your right. Quickly leave by rising left up the steep bank to an outer wall corner. Now bear away from the wall, rising gently to a brow with a ladder-stile to your right. Ignoring this, drop to a gate in a wall just ahead. Joining an access road, this will lead all the way back.

Turn right on a steady rise alongside grassy moorland to Ash Hill on the brow. A firm, unsurfaced road continues in the same style between pasture and wall, commencing a sustained, very gentle decline with good verges and a wall alongside. When a drive drops right to West Common Top Farm, the way improves into a gentler cart track with a series of intervening gates as fields take over alongside. The track improves still further as it leads down to emerge alongside the visitor centre, which had already appeared long in advance.

Wynch Bridge

15 HOLWICK SCARS

4 miles from Bowlees

An intriguing exploration of the many features around a remote Upper Teesdale settlement

Start Visitor centre (NY 906281; DL12 OXF), car park off B6277
Map OS Explorer OL19, Howgill Fells & Upper Eden Valley & OL31, North Pennines - Teesdale & Weardale

Based in an old Methodist chapel, Bowlees visitor centre is run by the North Pennines AONB, with refreshments, a small shop and WC. It is linked to the car park by a footbridge on Bow Lee Beck. With your back to the visitor centre, head away past cottages on your left to the main road. Just yards right, a gate opposite sends a firm path across two fields to the wooded environs of the River Tees. Pass through the stile and descend to Wynch Bridge. This suspension bridge dates from 1830, its predecessor being built to serve lead miners. Immediately upstream is lovely Low Force.

From the bridge go left to a kissing-gate, and head away from the river on a path running to a tiny stone-arched bridge. Across, rise to a wall-stile then more faintly up the field to another. Rising gently again, Holwick Scars appear ahead as you join an unfenced road. Go right, over a cattle-grid at Low Pikestone and on beneath trees sheltering Holwick Lodge. Ignore a left fork to the Earl of Strathmore's 19th century shooting lodge, and remain on this road as it becomes rougher to run through several fields to approach Hield House. Rising to the farm, through the last gate before it take an inviting grass track curving left to a solitary barn in a dip. Just behind it is a gate into open country. A grass track rises directly away, winding up to soon fade by an old sheepfold. Now rise right to a gate in the fence just above. A thin but clear path rises gently right into juniper bushes, forging a grooved course up The Bands.

Towards the top the path escapes left up onto a grassy knoll, with fenced enclosures to your left and above. Rise to that above, passing outside it to its right. From the top corner the path picks up again to vacate the juniper and rise thinly but clearly to veer gently right to a fence-stile onto the open moor. Just behind it is a hard shooters' track: turn left for an easy stroll on broad grass verges. Joined by another track and then by a wall, it drops down to dramatically reveal the Whin Sill cliffs of Holwick Scars ahead. In front of them the track drops stonily left the short way to a hairpin bend. Leaving the track's descent to Holwick Lodge, take a sheep-sculpture stile/gate in front. An inviting track heads away to drop into splendid ravine-like surrounds. On easing out it breasts a minor brow before slanting down to leave the moor by a house, with a short access road running to the road in Holwick.

Bear right beneath the scars through the scattered settlement, the most northerly in Yorkshire's historic North Riding. Reaching a stile on the left at School House, note that just a little further down the road is the Strathmore Arms: almost next door is a farmhouse eatery. From the stile head down the length of the field, joining a fading grassy track to a stile/gate left of two barns. Gently down the next long field, bear right to a corner stile onto the Tees' bank just above Scoberry Bridge. Turn upstream on a firm path with the lively Tees, its enchanting waterplay leading back to Wynch Bridge to finish as you began.

Holwick Lodge from Holwick Scars

16 HIGH FORCE

4¾ miles from High Force

Teesdale's highlight is at the heart of stunning scenery

Start High Force Hotel
(NY 885286;
DL12 0XH), car park
Map OS Explorer OL31,
North Pennines - Teesdale & Weardale (or OL19)

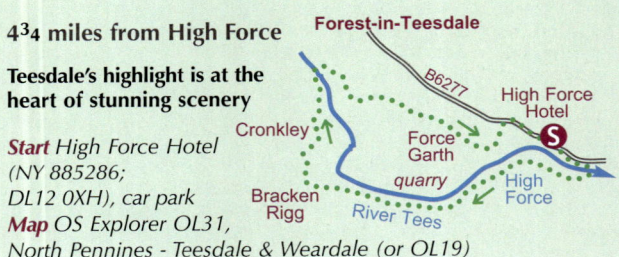

Return to the road and go left for no more than 100 yards to a path on the right into trees, with the River Tees below. After a brief slant, stone steps descend into a beautiful riverside pasture. Turn briefly downstream to Holwick Head Bridge, a footbridge. Across, turn right on a firm path into colourful terrain dominated by juniper. After an early kissing-gate you become disconnected from the river, but before long reach a tiny branch right to a viewing platform. Here, in all its glory, the magnificent High Force crashes down into its rocky basin. After suitable appreciation, resume along the well-made path, emerging via a kissing-gate above the top of the falls: extreme care is needed if peering down! Upstream, the path enters a super upland setting above the peerless river. An old wall precedes a footbridge on Blea Beck, where look back upstream to the waterfall of Bleabeck Force. Just before this the immense Force Garth Quarry has appeared on the opposite bank, though soon fades from the scene. Across a stile the path runs through a lush green pasture away from the river, to meet it again at successive footbridges on twin sidestreams.

The path now slants away from the river, rising between fenced juniper zones onto Bracken Rigg. With the river in view to the right, you gain a brow marked by two stone guideposts. Bear right, a flagged section descending to a stile near the corner, then rising with a wall to a fence-gate on a brow. Still flagged, it runs on with the wall to a stile in it. A brief narrow section opens out to reveal the river again beyond the farm at Cronkley below. The super little path slants down this colourful enclosure, dropping to a bridle-gate in the bottom corner. From a stile/gate behind, an enclosed section rises to a bridle-gate at the farm. Without entering, skirt left around a large modern barn to a bridle-gate onto the access road: go left to cross Cronkley Bridge on the river.

Remain on the track as it swings right over a cattle-grid and along to rise to another. Over it, leave by a gate on the right and advance towards isolated Hill End, but swing left before it with the wall to a corner stile. Now slant left up rough pasture, joining a grassy way rising to run to a gate in a wall ahead. A splendid grassy way heads away, with a wall and a craggy escarpment to your right. Gently rising to a brow advance on, and as the way forks keep right. As it later bears off left remain with the wall, and a little further, another grass track comes in at a gate to continue to a gate at the end. Joining a firmer cart track, this runs on with a wall to arrive above a cottage, and joined by its access road runs the short way further to East Force Garth. From a gate into the farmyard pass right of the buildings and down the stony drive onto the quarry access road. Turn left back onto the B6277, and a footway leads you quickly back to the start.

By the Tees above High Force

17   LANGDON BECK

4 miles from Forest-in-Teesdale

Magnificent upper dale scenery from riverbank to moor-edge pastures

Start Hanging Shaw (NY 867298; DL12 0HA), car park on old road
Map OS Explorer OL31, North Pennines - Teesdale & Weardale

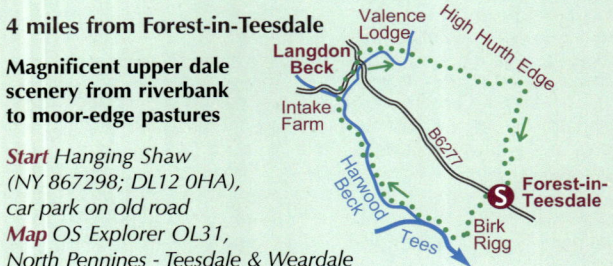

The scattered community of Forest-in-Teesdale is named after the vast hunting forest of the Baliols. Head north on the main road for 100 yards then turn down a driveway on the left to Birk Rigg. Already you have a magnificent prospect of Cronkley Scar with extensive high fells beyond. Pass to the right outside a shed and on to a gateway just ahead, then descend a slim enclosure to a wall-stile. Continue down to a barn, then briefly left with the wall to a corner gate. Go right the short way to a gate ahead, then left with the fence, becoming a wall dropping onto a rough road. Just ahead you meet the River Tees at Cronkley Bridge. Don't cross but turn upstream for a grand stroll by the wide-flowing river, passing through a kissing-gate to squeeze beneath Haugh Hill. A little further is a confluence with Harwood Beck, which is traced unfailingly upstream to a farm road at Saur Hill Bridge.

Across, a bridle-gate on the right sends a thin path to a stile into a beckside pasture. Advance on until rising up a bank, and a fence leads on to a corner. Over to the right is the church of St James the Less, with the white-walled dwellings of Langdon Beck ahead. From a bridle-gate on the right, double back a few yards to find a path slanting down the bank and running upstream to approach Intake Farm. Ending at a bridle-gate into a small enclosure, cross to a gate by the house: keep right on a short path between garden and beck to a concrete crossing onto a road. Here Langdon Beck joins Harwood Beck: go right with the former for a few minutes to the B6277 at Langdon Beck Hotel, highest pub in Teesdale.

Leave almost at once on a narrow lane opposite the pub. Passing between barns, it traces the beck to the farm at Valence Lodge. Enter the yard and bear right after the house to a bridge on the beck. A stony track winds up to quickly ease, then swings grassily left up to a gate in a wall. Entering large rough pasture, bear right on a quad track just above the wall, and above a barn bear further left, now pathless up the reedy pasture to the base of a grassy spoil heap. Behind it is a ruined hut and a lead mine level. Massive views look over the dale past Cronkley Scar overtopped by Mickle Fell.

A thin trod runs the short way right to a fence-stile, from where slant up across the part-moist field to a gate in the wall opposite. Slant up again to the opposite wall, then rise left to a gate at the far end, above a corner and just beneath the limestone scar of High Hurth Edge. Located within these scars, Teesdale Cave was excavated to reveal bones of lynx and wolf. Through the gate cross a streamlet, and a level grassy way heads away to the sharp bend of a firmer cart track. Turn right down this for an extended descent through rough pastures. Entering a field it becomes stony for the final stage down to Forest, winding more sharply down to the first house. Go left down the rough access road to emerge alongside the tiny school, with the start just below.

Cronkley Fell from the River Tees

18 CAULDRON SNOUT

3¾ miles from Cow Green Reservoir

An interesting mix of tarmac nature trail leading to contrastingly rugged waterfalls in a magnificent setting

Start Weelhead Sike (NY 810309; DL12 0HX), car park at end of minor road from B6277 at Langdon Beck
Map OS Explorer OL31, North Pennines - Teesdale & Weardale

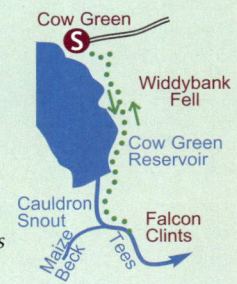

As recently as 1971, Cow Green Reservoir flooded a great upland basin to supply industry on Teesside. 770 acres in extent and with a capacity of 9,000,000,000 gallons, its construction had botanists on hands and knees to rescue rare and precious alpine plants. Unchanged, at least, is the western skyline of the Pennine giants of Mickle Fell, Meldon Hill, Great Dun Fell, Little Dun Fell and Cross Fell. At a lofty 1673ft/510m, the start point is only a few feet beneath the walk's summit. National Nature Reserve information leaflets are usually available, as is a summer WC.

From the information panels at the top of the car park head back along the road a short way, and as it swings left signs point you along a firm path to the right. This runs a straight course to quickly meet a track, where go briefly left to meet the surfaced Birkdale Farm access road at a gate/kissing-gate in a fence. Pass through and head away for a lengthy stroll along the road, this dubbed a nature trail of which the leaflet gives much information. Passing an early fenced mineshaft and then a weather station on a brow (the walk's summit), a pronounced drop crosses Red Sike before dropping to the end of the dam. This concrete monstrosity desecrates the very heart of magnificently remote upland country: it was none other than the legendary fellwalker A Wainwright who lamented "Surely the beautiful Tees, of all northern rivers, was born to run free". The massive dam is 1875ft long and 82ft high, and the humiliated Tees gushes out of a pipehcle at its foot. The road descends to meet the Pennine Way at a bridge on the revived river.

The walk suddenly transforms here as you leave just before the bridge to reveal the top of Cauldron Snout almost immediately below you. An initially moist, crazy-paved path heads away to the crest of the falls, then commences a cautious descent. Obviously you could choose to survey it from above and then opt to head back. Ideally follow the path crossing boulders and slabs down its side, with caution being needed. Part way down at a fork the briefly level left branch might be taken for an easier descent to the foot of the waterfall. Relax on the grassy sward at the base of the falls to savour this magnificent situation. Ideally, continue on the grassy path the few minutes away to the confluence of Maize Beck with the Tees, another grand spot to linger To your left downstream are the archetypal Whin Sill outcrops of Falcon Clints.

To return, take the main path from the foot of the falls and remain on it, closer to the action as the way scrambles up the stepped columns that fringe the falls: care is needed not to gawp too much when you should be watching your step. The aura of this magical place is sadly somewhat tainted when sufficient height has been regained to reveal the daunting appearance of the dam. On joining the road simply retrace steps to the car park.

The Tees at Cauldron Snout

19 WEARHEAD

4 miles from Cowshill

The highest walk in Weardale combines mining remains with superb views and a lovely riverbank

Start Village centre (NY 855406; DL13 1JQ), car park
Map OS Explorer OL31, North Pennines - Teesdale & Weardale

Some 1230ft/375m up, Cowshill is a typical Upper Weardale community, with St Thomas' church and the Cowshill Hotel. An old milestone points to the market towns of Alston and Allendale. To the west at Killhope is the North of England Lead Mining Museum. From the central bridge on Sedling Burn, with a waterfall upstream, a rough road leaves the sharp bend to its right. This runs to a gate/stile by a house into the open country of the former Sedling Lead Mine, part of the largest mining area in Weardale. Advance with the burn on your left, rising gently until levelling on reaching a fork opposite a lone house over to your left. The right fork takes you a few yards further to a gate in the adjacent wall.

An inviting grass track winds uphill alongside the deep groove of Sedling Vein. Great views look back over village and mine site, with Burnhope Reservoir across the main valley. Higher, it zigzags before rising more stonily to a gate in the wall at the top. The track continues rising with the wall, with old workings on your left. Finally easing out, it runs to the walk's summit at a gate at converging walls. Through it, turn right through a gate just below. A splendid descent commences on a wallside path, down to a corner gate and resuming with a wall on your left. This drops to a gate just above isolated Halliwell House. A cart track continues down, joined by a firmer access road a little short of a gate at the bottom onto a back road. Go left, dropping to a junction where turn right for a steep descent into the hamlet of West Blackdene.

Across Blackdene Bridge a gate on the right sends a short access road to Waterside Farm. From a gate into the yard, pass straight through to a gate onto a lovely riverbank. The path heads away across several field centres close by the river, later passing a wall-end to a pair of small gates preceding a final, tightly enclosed riverbank section to the bridge at Wearhead. This small village was terminus of the Wear Valley Railway which arrived here in 1895. Across the bridge is a WC, while several houses feature former shop fronts. Advance along the street until just past the village hall of 1900, then turn left down an access road towards the school.

Over the bridge, a gate on the right sends a grassy track away. Quickly fading, bear right to a fence by the river to see a pair of little waterfalls. Through an adjacent wall-stile, head upstream through a long pasture to a stile at the end. Resuming, shortly bear left to a kissing-gate in a wall outside a lone house. Bear left onto a minor knoll, and from the wall corner there a little path heads away with the wall. At the far end you join the driveway for the last few strides onto a road on the village edge. Go right over the twin-arched bridge then sharp right on an access road between houses, with the church just above. At a bend at a bridge on Sedling Burn with a waterfall below, don't cross but go left along a cottage front to steps sending a short path between wall and ravine up to a stile back into the centre.

The Wear below Wearhead

20 IRESHOPEBURN

3¾ miles from St John's Chapel

A leisurely mix of riverside rambling and open views from gentle slopes

Start Village centre (NY 884379; DL13 1QF), parking area by auction mart
Map OS Explorer OL31, North Pennines - Teesdale & Weardale

St John's Chapel is the hub of uppermost Weardale, with its setted little market place, shop, Post office, café, WC and St John's church. The Town Hall of 1865 sits on a green, with the Golden Lion and Blue Bell pubs close by. The Weardale Show takes place in August. From the green follow the side road behind the town hall down to a junction, where go left over Harthope Burn. With the school on your left, go right along a short access road to a kissing-gate into a field. Crossing the course of the old railway, a path bears away left to a footbridge across the lively River Wear. It heads directly away to a path crossroads at a wall corner: turn left to commence a level stroll on a field-path linked by stiles or kissing-gates. At an early split go straight ahead, and at the end a fence leads on to a stile/gate onto an access track at Island House.

Go straight across on a short cart track, then cross a small bridge into a few trees, with a kissing-gate in front and another just behind it. Now with the Wear again, a fieldside path runs above its tree-lined course to a stile. At the far end a stile/gate put you onto a stony access road. Ignoring the adjacent footbridge, go straight ahead to a delightful waterfall. Continue past it on a good path between river and wall, all the way to Coronation Bridge, commemorating Victoria's coronation in 1837. Ireshopeburn is just across it, with the Weardale Museum at historic High House Chapel. Nearby is Weardale Adventure Centre with cafe.

Cross the road, not the bridge, and resume on the riverbank. Passing beneath a concrete bridge you join a hard track from it, this access road leading along to a lone house before reaching the hamlet of West Blackdene. Turn left over Blackdene Bridge and along the road, bridging the old railway to a T-junction with the A689. Go left on the footway to the edge of Ireshopeburn. At the bridge on Ireshope Burn take a short-lived access track right, ending at a house to continue as a streamside path onto a road.

Go left over the bridge and take a gate by a house on the right. Your objective is a wall-stile in the far top corner of the field where wall and fence meet. Joining a road, climb steeply right to a junction, where keep left. Soon easing, it rises again to the start of a plantation. A grassy track slants left down through the trees to a gate into a field. The onward track bears left to a gateway opposite, then more sharply left to fade before a bottom corner gate in front of High Hotts. Pass between the buildings to a gate back out, and commence a level stroll through several fields. Entering a larger one with a reedy hollow, as you approach the wall go left with it to a corner stile. Now slant gently right down above a fence to a corner gate at High Prys. Joining its drive this leads down to the road, but at a sharp bend left cut a corner by using a fence-stile in front, then down the wallside towards a house. A small gate before it sends you down its outside to a wall-stile back onto the A689 on the village edge. Go right on the footway back into the centre.

The Wear above St John's Chapel

21 MIDDLEHOPE BURN

$3^1{}_2$ miles from Westgate

Exploring waterfalls and lead mining remains in a fascinating side valley

Start *Village centre (NY 908380; DL13 1RX), layby opposite caravan site*
Map *OS Explorer 307, Consett & Derwent Reservoir & Explorer OL31, North Pennines - Teesdale & Weardale*

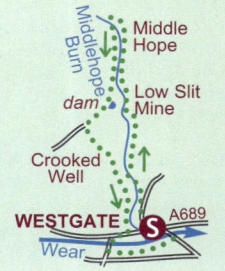

The tidy village of Westgate stands where Middlehope Burn enters the River Wear. Here are the Hare & Hounds pub, a caravan site and the site of a 14th century pele tower. From the centre turn up the Rookhope road, and at a former chapel of 1791, go left on a short access road to a gate into Slitt Wood. Just past the former High Mill, a kissing-gate sends a super path into the dene of Middlehope Burn, commencing with beautiful waterfalls. After further falls the excellent path runs on for a considerable time, twice bridging the beck and passing beneath a limestone cliff. After another waterfall a kissing-gate puts you into a lead mining site, with bunkers where lead ore was stored. Just a little further is the substantial Low Slit Mine, with a host of interesting features.

The path resumes upstream through scattered trees, a lovely stroll emerging at a kissing-gate into the more open surrounds of Middle Hope. More limestone scars precede lesser remains at Middlehope Shield Mine, and a grassy path slants down into open terrain. Passing a linear pond and an arched level, a kissing-gate puts you into the site of Middlehope Mine, with ruins on the other bank. The right of way shadows the old wall on your right to join a track which winds down left past an arched level to ford the stream at the walk's turning point.

The track doubles back to climb to a gate above, but leave virtually at once on a little path downstream beneath the wall. Part way along take a stile in it, and a broad grassy way traces the course of a mineral railway. This runs to a tumbledown stile then rises slightly to run level again, over a dam embankment and on to a stile at West Slit Dam. Advance on the embankment path ahead, at the end swinging right a little more faintly to a gate behind pens onto the head of a road. Turn immediately left by a barn, through a gate and down an access track to High Crooked Well. Continue straight past it down the fields to end at Low Crooked Well. From a kissing-gate to its left, descend to a kissing-gate below, down past a ruinous barn and all the way to the rear of farm buildings and houses at Weeds. Through a bottom corner gateway drop to a gate into the yard, and out on the access road into the village.

For a nicer finish, go right past an imposing Methodist Chapel and then left on a narrow road down to a concrete ford and sturdy footbridge on the River Wear. Across, pass the old rail bridge site to a kissing-gate on the left. Head away to another, then the way forks. The right of way heads straight on above the wooded bank in front, through another kissing-gate to one in the far corner. An alternative path drops left to follow the course of the railway by the river beneath a low wooded bank, then on into the open and along to meet the right of way at a few steps up onto a road. Go left over the bridge back into the village centre.

Low Slit Mine

22 ROOKHOPE ARCH

3³⁄4 miles from Rookhope

Moorland and lead mining in the upper Rookhope valley

Start *Village centre (NY 938429; DL13 2BG), roadside parking, car park at village hall*
Map *OS Explorer 307, Consett & Derwent Reservoir*
Access *Open Access (tiny section)*

    For a note on Rookhope see page 50. From the war memorial just over the bridge past the pub, take an access road past Boltsburn Mine House rising steeply to meet a stony access road. Go left up this through a gate onto open ground, ignoring a left branch before swinging left towards a house. Quickly leave by a kissing-gate just above, and a path slants up to a gate onto the foot of the moor. Rising left to a fence corner, follow it left. Quickly becoming a wall, the main path slants gently right as a broader grassy way up to spoil heaps at a recolonised quarry. The path contours on to a wall corner, on above the wall and a house at Redburn to join its drive. Go briefly right, and as it climbs away, take a grassy path straight ahead. This quickly slants left down to a wall with a mast behind. Go briefly right to the wall corner on a broader grassy way, picking up another just below and out onto a road just ahead. Drop left past Bankfoot Cottage and over a bridge to a cattle-grid.
    Immediately across take a gate on the right, and ignoring the track rising away, bear left onto a broad, faint grassy way running left near a fence. At the end it swings right, but you drop the short way to a gate onto a road opposite Rookhope Arch. At the site of Rookhope Smelt Mill, it is the last survivor of six that straddled the road to the foot of a long chimney that took fumes away. Go right to turn left on the bridge on Rookhope Burn, and rise briefly to a gate on the left. This sends a grassy track winding down to view the arch. Leaving, slant back to a level grassy track from the gate, running the short way to a footbridge on the burn.

Don't cross but turn right up a path at the rear of a cottage, and onto its short drive up to a junction. Go left, turning for a short, steep climb to level out beneath grassy moor. Rapidly forking, take the left branch to a gate, and with Lintzgarth Farm ahead, fork right to a gate, then dropping the short way to Saughtree Cottage. From a bridle-gate to its left pass round its outbuilding, then slant right down to a corner stile beneath a gate. Cross the field to a stile opposite, then bear left to a gate opposite. A longer slant leads to a corner stile right of Broad Dale House. Cross the lawn to a stile opposite, and a grassy way descends past a derelict house with Rookhope below. At the bottom is a stile into a small industrial site. Dropping briefly down, turn right on a wide rough road along the front of a works unit: this is the course of the Rookhope & Middlehope Railway which served lead mines above Westgate.

Forge on through an old site with new tree plantings. At the end is a stand of trees on the right, with a gate in front, and the improving line continues towards a cutting. However, this is also the point to leave, dropping left to a defunct stile with a gateway to its left. Drop down the bank to reveal a lone house below, and down to a stile into its grounds. Go left past the house on your left to a gate accessing the burn. Go left a few strides to a footbridge across it, and an enclosed path heads away past a graveyard, at the end rising right onto the road. Go left into the village edge, with a footway back through to the centre.

Rookhope Arch

23 BOLTSLAW INCLINE

4 miles from Rookhope

Richly varied moorland walking above a sleepy side valley

Start Village centre (NY 938429; DL13 2BG), roadside parking, car park at village hall
Map OS Explorer 307, Consett & Derwent Reservoir
Access Open Access, see page 4

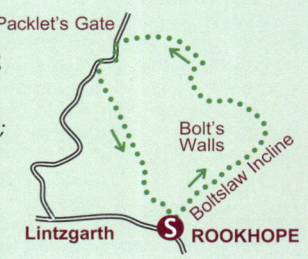

Rookhope stands at a lofty 1082ft/330m at the heart of its own side valley above Weardale. The main settlement has the Rookhope Inn, Post office/shop, Wesleyan Methodist Chapel of 1865 and WC. Holy Trinity church stands to the south, and you can even go alpaca trekking. The 19th century saw Rookhope buzz to the sound of railways, with a line running south-west to lead mines above Westgate. It then climbed out of the valley via the 2000 yards-long Boltslaw Incline which hauled waggons onto the moortops for the onward shipment of lead and quarried limestone. Additionally, a short line ran west to Rookhope Smelt Mill at Lintzgarth (see Walk 22).

From the bend by the shop and WC turn up the access road to Hylton Terrace. Climbing steeply, ignore side branches to level out and run left to a gate onto grassy moorland. Within yards you join the route of the Boltslaw Incline rising from the left (named from the hilltop summit of Bolt's Law). This points you in a direct line up the moorland flank, with an excellent grass verge. With a cairn sat atop spoil heaps on the skyline just ahead (and the remains of Boltslaw engine house just beyond, rise to within two minutes of it before branching left on an inviting grassy track.

This contours on for a splendid, long half-mile above the slopes of Bolt's Walls and through a row of shooting butts. A short drop precedes an equal rise to resume level, soon becoming less bold and bearing right. Rising slightly, it passes another line of butts then bears further right on a more defined rise. Briefly narrowing to a trod, it broadens again to double back left and level out before reaching a junction. Go left for another grand near-level stride that runs around to join an open moor road just beneath Packlet's Gate. Go left downhill to swing in around Stogel Clough, emerging to reach a footpath sign on the left. This sends a thin but clear trod slanting down through heather, quickly easing to commence an extended, very gentle descent of the moorland flank. Intermittently level, it is at times fainter than others but should be easily traceable, helped by occasional marker posts.

Largely leaving heather behind, it continues down to eventually reach the last marker on a minor knoll. Resume down to a small spoil heap now serving as a rabbit warren, with the village now just below. The path drops gently right to the wall just below, turning left with it and continuing with a fence to its corner. Here the path slants right over a plank bridge down to a corner gate off the moor. The path continues down a rough enclosure to a kissing-gate onto an access road. Go left, curving down over open ground to a kissing-gate above a gate, just beneath which it forks. Go right, dropping steeply down past cottages to emerge by Boltsburn Mine House at the war memorial.

On Boltslaw Incline

24 ROOKHOPE BURN

3¹⁄4 miles from Eastgate

A quiet side valley offers relaxing walking amid farming dereliction

Start *Village centre (NY 952387; DL13 2HW), village hall car park*
Map *OS Explorer 307, Consett & Derwent Reservoir*

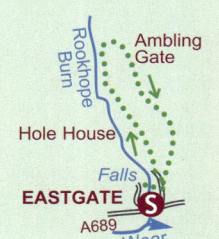

Tiny Eastgate stands where Rookhope Burn joins the River Wear, and has the Cross Keys pub, All Saints church and a former Wesleyan Chapel of 1891. Closure of its massive cement works in 2002 devastated the local economy: it was served by the similarly defunct railway until 1993. A sheep show takes place in May. From the pub cross the bridge on Rookhope Burn and turn left up the road past the chapel and church. Opposite the village hall (former school) take a tiny detour left to visit the waterfalls: from the short access road go right in front of a house, down outside its grounds to a footbridge on the burn. To your right is Low Linn, the lower of a pair of delightful waterfalls. The higher Donter Linn is also visible, falling into a deep, circular pool.

Back on the narrow lane, resume steeply uphill to ease out above the wooded bank dropping to the stream. A stile on your right is the point to which you will return, but for now resume along the level road. Passing Holme House it continues with nice valley views to end at Hole House. From the right-hand gate at the end a path slants up through trees at Ashy Bank, a steady rise to a gateway into a field. Advance on above the wooded bank, and when the fence drops away, slant gently down towards the stream. Dropping past a wall corner, don't join the stream but turn right along the slope, a grassy way soon becoming clearer beneath an old wall end. As it runs on through the surrounds of Ambling Gate Bank, you will have realised that the wood shown on the map is non-existent. The way forges pleasantly on, dropping to the lively burn beneath power lines. A broader, part rushy pasture leads on through a moister section to a footbridge on Brandon Clough.

This is your turning point, so don't cross but turn right up the streamside. Soon narrowing, a path forms for a short, steep rise, bearing right up to a gate where a fence meets a wall. Head away with the wall, through an intervening gate and along to the farm at Ambling Gate. A corner gate puts you onto the drive: turn into the yard on this, and on past the farmhouse on your right to a gate into a field. A grass track crosses to a gate ahead, then slants gently right down to another. The track runs with a wall on your right to a forest of nettles at the scant ruins of Burnt Walls. Continue straight on the fading track above the wall, through three further fields to a gate accessing the romantic ruin of Ashy Bank.

Enter the yard at the rear to a wall-stile out. Cross to another and on to a ladder-stile in a collapsing wall. Now bear right to the wall ahead (gap left of blocked stile), then on to a corner stile/gate beneath an old barn. Cross to a wall ahead and bear right with it, down through an old wall. Slanting left, drop more steeply down over a grass track to a rickety corner gate. With a wall to your left, slant down this large pasture to a bottom corner stile/gate. Joining the road on which you began, go left to finish.

The Cross Keys, Eastgate

25 STANHOPE BURN

4¾ miles from Stanhope

Heather moors and old industry in and around Stanhope Dene

Start *Village centre (NY 996391; DL13 2PZ), ample parking*
Map *OS Explorer 307, Consett & Derwent Reservoir*

Access *Open Access, see page 4*

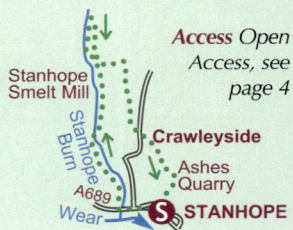

Capital of Weardale, busy little Stanhope has the Durham Dales Centre, St Thomas' church, Stanhope Castle and shops, pubs and cafes. From the setted square head west on the A689, and just over Stanhope Burn bridge take an access road right past imposing Stanhope Old Hall. Quickly ending at a house, a path goes right with the burn into Stanhope Dene. Before an early footbridge fork left up to a little gate. Now enclosed, it swings right along a field bottom to the top of a wood where it rises gently along the edge. Towards the end fork right, dropping slightly and along to the wood edge, where it resumes outside. Before the wood end, fork right to run to an inner wood corner and resume along the top. Further, the path slants down to a footbridge over the burn.

Ascend steps in front onto an access road and take a level stroll left above the burn, passing old quarries to reach derelict buildings at the site of Stanhope Smelt Mill. At further buildings just beyond, the track swings left to bridge the burn. Ignore this and take a gate in front onto heathery moor. Of two paths heading away keep left, going straight ahead just above the stream. Past the odd minor landslip it runs more easily on, from heather to rushes to bracken as it forges on close by the stream. After the wall opposite departs, continue for a further five minutes until the path meets the beck for the second time since the wall departed, with a big bouldery hollow higher on your flank just ahead.

This is your turning point, so double back around 60 yards to locate a slim path slanting up through heather. Once discerned it slants steadily out of bracken to join a clearer level path. Go right for a super stride, broadening considerably to arrive above where you entered the moor. When a right fork drops to it, keep straight on towards a wood corner. A slimmer short-cut slants left to join a track climbing from the gate. This ascends the wallside past old quarries to where the wall drops away: take a green way slanting down with it to cross Heathery Burn. The path resumes with the wall climbing away, levelling out to trace it across grassy moor (ignoring a left branch) to reach the far corner. From a gate on the right, go left by sheep pens to a corner bridle-gate behind. It then traces the wallside to a bridle-gate onto a road at Crawleyside. Tunnelling beneath here was a rail incline that hauled limestone up from Ashes Quarry and over the moors to Consett steelworks.

From a gate opposite, a path heads right across moorland, briefly with a fence then wall, then striding on through heather. At a fork a thinner path slants right down to a fence, then left down to a kissing-gate in it. From another just below, a lush path drops left through bracken to a fenceside path overlooking the immense former Ashes Quarry. Go left, curving right at the end with the fence down to a kissing-gate and a pair of improbable footbridges over the old site. Continue down a track to a cross-paths, and down to a kissing-gate where it runs enclosed down onto Chapel Street in Stanhope. Go left past a Methodist church as far as the first road right, then down past the church to finish.

At Stanhope Burn

26 BOLLIHOPE LANDSCAPES

4½ miles from Bollihope

Two moorland strolls on splendid old ways amid remains of old industries

Start Bollihope Bridge (NZ 006349; DL13 2SZ), large parking area on north side
Map OS Explorer OL31, North Pennines - Teesdale & Weardale

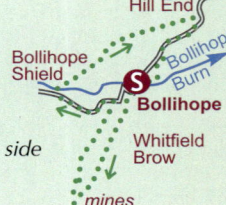

Cross the bridge to the south side, and bear left up a broad grassy way through bracken to join an access road. Just over to the left is a mine 'shop' where leadminers at the nearby crushing mill lodged during their working week. Continue up the road, and when it loses its surface and swings left to the houses of Whitfield Brow, advance straight on a stony access road. This rises briefly then levels out for a lengthy stroll above the deep, bracken-draped Howden Burn, largely with a grass verge. At the end you enter the Cornish Hush Lead Mines site, with a small arched level beneath a landslip on your left, and a watercourse emerging. Just past it the track crosses the beck for a short rise to the level former mine site.

Just a little further ahead the track re-crosses the stream, but here you turn around by doubling back right up through a few reeds, passing right of a small pool and up into heather. This less than ideal stage is very brief, and easing out, a grassy way should be found to rise very slightly as it runs the short way to a wall corner ahead. By now very clear, the path runs on the wallside, and when the wall drops away the path commences a gentle descent of the grassy moor with big open views. Closing in on your start point, it meets a track at a wall corner for the short drop onto the road. With the start just two minutes to the right, your onward route goes left with the road for ten minutes, largely with neat verges to the lone house at Camperdown.

Immediately after it, turn right down the short farm road to Bollihope Shield. Across the burn and into the yard, pass left of the house and around to a gate in the wall behind. Re-entering open moorland, a super green way slants up to the right above a splendid double kiln arrangement. The way then swings left to commence a sustained slant up across the increasingly heathery moor, revealing your start point beneath fine open views. Your path becomes less bold but never in doubt, gaining the upper flank to level out and run beneath the crest to join a firm track in front of a clump of reeds.

Turn right on this for a magnificent, long level stride on a largely grassy surface. At the end it forks in front of a clump of trees within the walled grounds of an isolated house above the hamlet of Hill End. Bear right around to the front to join a rough access road dropping right onto a road. Turn right for a long, steady slant back down to the start, with a lush verge the whole way. Just after the nearby wall drops away, a nicer finish takes a broad grassy way dropping left through bracken, then steeply down to a stony access road just short of the burn. With some very distinctive remains of quarrying opposite, turn right for two minutes back to the start.

Bollihope Burn

27 TUNSTALL RESERVOIR

4¾ miles from Tunstall

Good paths and heather moorland high above an attractive reservoir

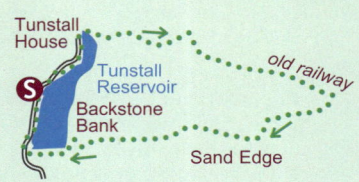

Start *Tunstall Reservoir (NZ 064413; DL13 3LZ), water company car park (signed 2½ miles north of Wolsingham up Leazes Lane)*
Map *OS Explorer 307, Consett & Derwent Reservoir*
Access *Open Access (tiny section)*

Tunstall Reservoir was completed in 1879, and the circuit of its shore is a popular short stroll. Tunstall Fly Fishers often dot the waters with their small boats. Back on the road turn right to briefly follow it towards the reservoir head. Shortly after an early bridge, a gate on the right sends a path above the shore. This runs nicely along to emerge at a kissing-gate onto a hard track dropping from Tunstall House Farm at the road end. Turn right over the bridge on the reservoir head, and through a gate the track commences an unremitting climb outside Quarry Wood, largely with good grassy verges. When the wood turns off, the track rises more gently to a sharp bend in front of a wall and a section of a former railway.

Just short of the bend, take a grassy track right the short way to a gate/stile in another wall. A broad green way heads away, but yours is the thin path rising gently left beneath the railway wall. This runs for a while before slanting up to run alongside it: the unseen line occupies a deep, wild cutting at this point. Through a gate in a fence, a broader continuation runs through heather moorland to a stile/gate in a wall. Through this you join the old line, suddenly transformed into a mercurial, embanked green way. A super stride leads on past an old quarry in a wooded ditch, shortly after which you reach a sturdy cairn. Directly below is your objective of an outer wall corner enclosing a field. Here leave the railway for a two-minute drop through heather to it. You could opt to remain on the line to the end, where a grassy track slants sharply back right down to the wall corner.

At the wall corner go right on the good track, dropping gently the short way to ford a streamlet amid bracken. Rising away, it swings left back to a corresponding wall corner, to then rise gently left through the heather of Sand Edge. Rapidly fading on levelling out, a continuing thin trod quickly reaches a grassy little way. Swing right here to the first of a line of circular grouse butts, and simply follow a splendid grassy track their full length. Gently rising on a dead-straight course past all nine butts, it leads to a ladder-stile off the moor in the wall just beyond.

A thin trod heads away through rough pasture, curving left up to a fence-stile near a gate. The thin way resumes at the same angle to a gentle brow, running on more broadly to fade just short of a gate in a wall ahead. Through it another super grassy track drops down a wallside into a third pasture, where a gate on the right sends it the short way to Backstone Bank Farm. Without entering, turn left down the steep access road with extensive valley views. Entering Backstone Bank Wood, a hairpin bend sends it down to arrive alongside the end of the dam. Across the outflow, a broad grassy verge shadows the road along to the valley road. Turn right, and just after the houses an old gate puts a path onto the shore, all the way back to the car park.

Tunstall Reservoir

28 — WEAR AT WOLSINGHAM

4½ miles from Wolsingham

Easy, level walking through grassy pastures

Start Village centre
(NZ 075372; DL13 3AB), car park
Map OS Explorer OL31, North Pennines - Teesdale & Weardale

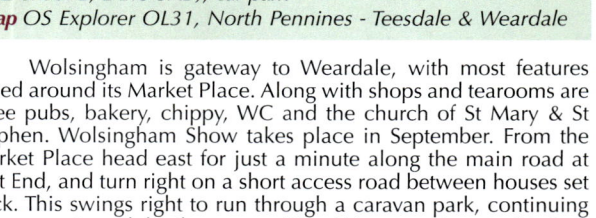

Wolsingham is gateway to Weardale, with most features based around its Market Place. Along with shops and tearooms are three pubs, bakery, chippy, WC and the church of St Mary & St Stephen. Wolsingham Show takes place in September. From the Market Place head east for just a minute along the main road at East End, and turn right on a short access road between houses set back. This swings right to run through a caravan park, continuing as a concrete path by the unseen River Wear to arrive at a big iron bridge. Don't pass under but turn briefly right to join the road, then left over the bridge above fine river scenery. Almost at once, before a railway bridge, a flight of steps on the right sends an enclosed path off between railway and river.

The Wear Valley Railway was completed in 1895, running 25 miles from Bishop Auckland to Wearhead. Passenger services ended in 1953, but the line served Eastgate cement works until 1993. The Weardale Railway now operates as a heritage line as far as Stanhope. At a kissing-gate into a field corner, a lengthy stroll begins parallel with the railway, though unfortunately the river is by now absent. A footbridge on a sidestream at the end puts you into an extremely long field with views up-dale. Over a small footbridge at the end the path becomes enclosed, and with a parallel permissive option, runs the short way with the river to join a road alongside a bridge. Turn right over the river and along to the main road, where go left on the verge for a few minutes.

Immediately after Halfway House on your left, take a stile on the right and bear left with a tree-lined streamlet. Bridging it in front of a gate at the end, pass through and ascend the fieldside on an embanked way. Through the top corner gate bear left to the far corner, then double back right on a dirt track to the corner ahead to meet the end of the embanked way. Through the gate keep right on the field edge, but at an early kink pass through a gate and resume with a fence on your right down to another early corner.

Through this gate bear left on the fence's other side, at once through another gate to begin a long, easy stroll back. Pathless underfoot, advance to a corner wall-stile ahead, and cross to a ladder-stile from where innumerable long but narrow field centres are crossed with stiles and the odd gate. Ths continual slight descent veers marginally right to ultimately reach a pair of gates. From the right one veer a little further right, and on to soon reach a kissing-gate where an enclosed path takes over. This runs outside school sports fields to emerge onto Leazes Lane on the village edge.

Go briefly right, then left at the entrance to a leisure centre. Keep to the path on the right to commence an enclosed, tarmac course to a bend in front of the church. Go straight ahead through the churchyard to a kissing-gate, from where a path slants left across a field to drop down a few steps into the car park. Ideally, first go left on a firm path the brief way upstream with Waskerley Beck to view some modest waterfalls at The Sills. Back at the car park, join the road and turn right back to the Market Place.

Wolsingham church

29   HAMSTERLEY FOREST

4¾ miles from Bedburn

Non-claustrophobic woodland is joined by beckside, moorland and green lane

Start Forestry England visitor centre (NZ 091312; DL13 3NL), car park
Map OS Explorer OL31, North Pennines - Teesdale & Weardale
Access Open Access, see page 4   (Explorer 305, few yards only)

    County Durham's largest forest has a visitor centre, café and WC, with popular mountain biking trails. With your back to the centre turn right along the surfaced road. A little after a Forest Drive road merges from the right, keep on a little further to where a broad forest road goes left. Before it bridges Bedburn Beck take a firm path right to rapidly rejoin the road, now with a footway. This runs the very short way with the beck to a public footpath signed left. The firm path now runs an enclosed course in close company with the beck, with open fields to your right. At the end the path crosses a footbridge on the sidestream of Ayhope Beck to enter a picnic area. Bear right on the firm path to rejoin the road.

    Turn right to re-bridge the beck, and just a little further past a house on the right. Here a path doubles back left alongside a small clearing with tables, then on into trees. Joining Ayhope Beck it runs an enjoyable, lengthy course, later leaving the stream and narrowing through bracken to reach a stony track alongside a low ruin and picnic tables. Turn right on this for a short, steep pull, over a level forest road and up to a gate onto open moorland. Go left on the continuing track, slanting up a groove outside the trees to reach the forest edge. The track continues rising, some sorry sections having been trashed by off-road vehicles. Easing out on the heathery moorland of Cabin Hill, big views look west over the trees to the long moorland skyline of Hamsterley Common.

A little higher the track swings right above a small quarried hollow: ignore a lesser left fork and continue on the main track, soon levelling to run a slowly improving course across the moor. On the brow to your left are quarried knolls, and ignoring a left branch you soon reach an outer wall corner containing the forest. The much-improved track runs on outside the trees, and when the wall drops away, it begins a steady slant left down to a gate off the moor. The enclosed grassy path of Stanhope Lane can be initially moist, but soon massively improves for a sustained, very steady descent between forestry and fields. Towards the bottom it enters more trees to emerge onto a road.

Turn right all the way to the bottom, passing a lodge and the forest entry point. Just past it is a lovely old millpond with a house on the left. Immediately past it is a parking area just before the bridge on Bedburn Beck. Turn right here along a short driveway to Field House. Without entering, a path diverts right outside its confines, over a stone slab bridge, around to a stile and second bridge into a field. A grassy path heads away, at the end joining the lively beck for an enclosed stroll upstream. Further, the path crosses a drain footbridge on your right to slant left across a field to a gate/stile back into the car park. *The millpond, Bedburn*

30 GRASSHOLME RESERVOIR

3½ miles from Grassholme

A simple circuit of an attractive sheet of water

Start Visitor centre (NY 948225; DL12 0PW), car park at south end of dam
Map OS Explorer OL31, North Pennines - Teesdale & Weardale
Access Water company permissive paths

Completed in 1915, Grassholme Reservoir is the lower of two in Lunedale, and covers some 140 acres. Opened in 1993, the visitor centre includes an exhibition along with information and WC. Popular for angling and watersports, also here is an observatory from where Teesdale's celebrated dark skies can be appreciated. From the lower car park the opening path heads away along the southern shore between the ever-present boundary wall and the water's edge. The wooded knoll of Kirkcarrion is seen back across the valley (see Walk 11). Encountering a couple of minor inlets, the latter stages see a broad, steeper bank form, and the main path is deflected left up onto it by a fence. This broad crest runs on high above the reservoir, and at the end it drops down two successive flights of wooden steps. A footbridge then points the path up to a kissing-gate onto Grassholme Lane.

Turn down to cross narrow Grassholme Bridge. In times of low water levels the old bridge re-appears in the upper section of the reservoir on the left, now designated a nature reserve. Much higher, not far beyond, is the grassy dam of Selset Reservoir, completed in 1960. Turn into a car park immediately across the bridge to commence your return along the north shore, more straightforward than the outer leg as it undulates along, again with a couple of minor inlets then a larger one. At the end cross the dam to finish, passing the old keeper's house.